T0108423

NATCH

CITY LIGHTS SPOTLIGHT SERIES NO. 20

SOPHIA DAHLIN

NATCH

CITY LIGHTS

SAN FRANCISCO

CITY LIGHTS SPOTLIGHT
The City Lights Spotlight Series was founded in 2009,
and is edited by Garrett Caples.

Library of Congress Cataloging-in-Publication Data
Names: Dahlin, Sophia, author.
Title: Natch / Sophia Dahlin.
Description: San Francisco, CA : City Lights Books, 2020.
Identifiers: LCCN 2020009380 | ISBN 9780872868106 (trade paperback)
Subjects: LCSH: Sexual minorities--Poetry. | Mind and body--Poetry. |
LCGFT: Poetry.
Classification: LCC PS3604.A3444 N38 2020 | DDC 811/.6--dc23
LC record available at https://lccn.loc.gov/2020009380

Cover art: Julio Linares, "Sophia" [detail] (2011), acrylic on cardboard.
Copyright © 2011 by Julio Linares

All City Lights Books are distributed to the trade by
Consortium Book Sales and Distribution: www.cbsd.com

For small press poetry titles by this author and others,
visit Small Press Distribution: www.spdbooks.com

City Lights Books are published at the City Lights Bookstore,
261 Columbus Avenue, San Francisco, CA 94133

www.citylights.com

CONTENTS

To my crushes

NATCH

PRISMR OF LOVE

I am all a lizard

plated muscle
adjusts and I like

I lick it

I like sunlight
deliberate

but scourge of the pallid
makes pink red

sours eyes
but my dizzied

my darling

whole lion

one wonders why am I
mugged or mugger

again my wallet sucks
my holes have holes halve

to avoid
to void to hole up

for a while w/baby
for the winter

a day's rubbery
that makes flowers dubious

and the ground glad
because an elastic life

it's an elastic life
because spring

like
combats the silvery

w/its temperature

till the summer fluster us
I let my rock

flex its muscle

which gleamy muscle's
me

I'M A NINNY

Someday my punishment will come
like a hamburger skidding down
a zinc countertop.

How still we'll be
me lollipopped on my paunchy stool
some bun stacked red with the glam of death
what was made for me is mine.

Oh last night the priest in the mirror said
You were lovely but you were bad
the doorhinge pinched my hand.

I sang *Who am I that ye condemn us*
the door *Pity pity babe repent*
thou'art flickering yet art thyself
I have not read the signs but have been told

whereto they jab. Hunger
or what I want to be hunger roils
in what I want to be my belly but

is not, I go forth ravenous and stay
out past the patience of my fellows
pivoting in the glow of the juke corner

humming on a buddy's shoulderblade, oh who'll
pity me if what undoes me is so nice.

If I'm warmed by heat that rises from my scrapes.

If my medicine is fetishes, you ask
where it hurts and my slow smile spoils my *There*

no cure for who I was but who I am.

TANDEM

I'll take a long view of the legs
and I'll readily endure them.

I will even hallow them, as a speaker-set,
I am actually tripping. I'm not,
but you see how some skins
go red-yellow-red-yellow? I was tripping
saying I could see all my fat and the blood cohabiting

but I could. The legs
take a stance, the legs have a pinion,
the legs make the ground distant. I'm kidding,
they're inside, it's floor. And I'm kidding,

I'm sitting. The chair makes the distance.
The legs blotch, like flypaper-pigment.
They're loudspeakers
today. Playing the cassette
of the cunt and its wishes.

I wish
they would play it more quiet.

The legs go hither and thither just blasting
the cunt's wants, like
you and you. You and you.
The cunt wants in twos. Or the legs
fathom binaries better?

They play loudly. And jigging with speed,
forgo unction, spraying
their reserves in the noon air,
so sun robs them midmotion.

This sun shows nothing new, the legs,
like all movers moved by a desiring engine,
and protracted desire devours treasure:
for example, wallets dry up on the dance floor.

But the legs come out upright.
I will allow them. Pillars to my deity.
Pinnacles for my nonpareil,
my succulent, all of a unity

paddles for the cleaved canoe,
breathes heady air from the legs' height,

it wants. I believe in the cunt,
I'll believe in the legs
later.

PONDER THE LILY HOW DOES IT GO

lilypads, how do they
touch us, slimy? we like
them speaking about the surfaces,
the sunlike either to build a catch
to see the pond floor past, or
the sun to make a mirror
to see the lily flowers each twice
how we like this nice difference,
switched lilies, the pad wired
subliminally to the pond floor, how
we get to be upstairs from ponds,
looking down like at a lily chandelier
top and to see the fish from here
glitzing like guests so we
are the privileged children to watch
them in their mysterious
lines that unseen move them along

I'll like to put my foot like lilypad
just on top of the view, wet

but not in, not washed but neat
and rest my lily weight on it
press the plane of not being there
but not being absent either, pond
and my pads and no print and chafes
the glass to repetitive protest yet
then is still yet not without response

SWITCH

why is it too obvious to slouch into the soft furniture
couch and sigh for power&fame! even my hands soften thinking
ah to be named even in my wig and shades
when small I thought the key might be to try
each thing then I thought no only one thing soon enough
I'll be "she who does thing" then
I sat on this couch.

oh it is gentle it is so gentle it
abrades me with its petting where I jut
gathers my gaze to this wall and the dry ice pouring
out the mantle (imagine if I had to housesit a house
the week before Halloween, imagine the cackling
doorway, cottony stair rail, vegetal exoskeletons

and the verdant witchy wagging her dick,
broom, her broomsdick, I want to watch out the window
daring the neighboring kids to name me "which"
I am the one "which one" this one "the window which"
this window and cast my shadow on the lawn)

now I have never had a lawn to spread out in but
have sat on couches, mine, and sofas of others, my
name means sofa in three languages and I am yours (which)
I wait for you, stuffed into posture

I'M A NATURAL

I'm going to have this
here

moment with the moon

in listening
to skimmed off light
of lake

I've found surfaces
of the most depth

but I think I'm who provides it
when I seal the lake
in sight

I get wet in the heart
and my eye is filling in

ripples
and a moon in me

the piercing
pussywillow
glances flat

the fish's nose
dull black

but the water holds
me in and a moon

LET GO SWIMMING

fairies are space
between us and natch

which is the most
invisible?

the mysterious, like
wet fire

where but it's air
full air

the full air between plants and people

feelings
on the leaf

or the sunset feelings

the thoughts of a mountain
puts a perspective

or how water makes it calm
like a sob is being done for us

all the glit
that outlines the silhouette

light is special

when there isn't a baby
the body is halfsies

it's not fairies

fairies are money

LEGROOM

because my lights go slip
I treasure my regrets

where the dial gets
really wide

where fingers fail
and the snowbank slinks to glass

green gestates
hesitantly
I can understand
terrified of being ice

but platefuls
of lispy salad greens

suggest idyllic patience with desire
a fielded
or a hilly wait

skirt peeping hopefulness
flipping the woolly folds

ease like a napping pilot
where the sea is dangerous

or like sex is dangerous
for the shepherdess

&VERSE TIPS TO THE SOUL LIKE COWS TO THE PASTURE

Living so vividly within her fears
has lost me to my own, her face
all overgrown with eyes.

But here my sun starts up
as guiltily as if caught sleeping, and my oceans
melt their caps in passing, and my men return
their shoesoles to the ground.

Living so open to her loveliness has knit me
flat upon my back to planet
open mouthed to air.

The sticky stars that complicate the night
in certain rural places I might go
to feel in company of my desire
will snag peaks of my skin.

Living within her mouth has coupled me
in echoes to my speech. The tall earth lilts me
trippily on prongs.

But I'm the lump in the snaking line.
Taking my legroom while I share a cab.
Her wide eyes whitening my path

her ululating thyroid, rubbery
erasing tongue.

ANYONE MUST SAND GINGERS

anyone must hide fingers
anyone must inhale and anyone must find noises
anyone must be staunch to sing a whale song
and one might lasso an outgoing bellow if one knew how
bring a woman ashore, bring a woman to sea
to ask is a fortune, anyone must read lightly

and embroider oblivion, anyone somewhere an angel
spoiling the make-up, must aspire to beacon
everlastingly flail for a chance in an angel ocean, and anyone
of substance must know it, any lingering chopsticks
toiling the green beans must glisten
anyone must invisibly coax

her squeaks from the woman, her mapping unlikely
inaccurate anyway losing its bends, what's a map
a proposal, anyone might make a bad turn
might put a wrong palm
up an ocean angelically frothing

a space must be canned
and rust bunch the hinge
anyone must burden
plain toast with some butter

BLUR ANISE

brunette thought of the scalp
I will brush it out because it's difficult
and prevents gleaming

when parts of a body seep
and other parts are civilized
how to usher up
panacea from the deep that won't unglue
hugs, that won't negate pats

rubicund bloom of the cooch, be still
or else be problematic, rivet
heat to the otherwise docile palm
fix its meandering

JK

Seasonal leaflessness. My neighborhood
has no lushes, only houses.

Reefs of kittens mewl at the crashing bush
and a cat whose body they got out of lies it
heavily upon them, or
my neighborhood

has no animals but the one I know by name
I gave. Night comes early for me, I steal seat
from patio steps and tile creeps

viney icy up. Nobody's not
old or young but me. But I'm gaining
pet of my ideal self,
that I've grown over again,

prettier, repetitively
romanced age thirty etc
what wholesome thing could excite me.

Who in my neighborhood sleeps
beneath bushes, no one I know.

Who bangs heartily at night, no one I know.
Knuckles douse the street in brine,
kittens collapse to powder,

my phone lights up with hideous
alacrity, or I devote
fun minutes to La Mom, or she isn't busy
strictly speaking honey. Who

in my neighborhood smokes in bed. Or likes
to cook alone. The aloof friend

of my future stirs
in the sky like Poppins,
winds of alteration.

PURCHASES

sweetheart please clamor, I am 100 aroused ears
quivering as if dispersed across a field
and I feel my foliage enlarging
rambling skyward in listening rhapsodic

eyes sliding neatly into the corner
where the sweetheart perches, daintily
visible, as fraught

as rain upon my fleshy area
or like we're in a cave, I wrote café
when the rain nips patrons from the sidewalk in

but I mean like we ranged on vacant rock
not knowing rain other than drips
you purge from stalactite
to stalagmite pointing ends

if I wrote tip it wd unfortunately rhyme
babeface leaf through me ungently as the researcher

who fears not library fines, bunch
my pages to extract
any info you could use

I mean to be mobile, I mean to rise startlingly
with your bouncing hand, no I mean to lie shudderingly
like stalks of waiting listeners and weeds
or be a brown bird gnarly in the sun

TIME CHECK

if the planets shift
next you'll probably get
very dreamy   if you are in
relationship you'll feel afloat
together   like a holding raft
and not awake
at all   you'll be aloft
on water or the air   whatever
pliant element   the couch
if your hair is long it will fall
if your back is bare
if your hair is high   will mat
when you take
a walk you'll find
yourself letting yourself walk
one block or two out of the route
not more   if you want or you'll enjoy
relief from the pressure of new
air   if you have a child
your shrugs

will frustrate them
you are evolving
if you know your father you will find
him on a porch and hang
out w/drinks   if you have ice
if you feel yourself
becoming stranger
howdy stranger
if you lapse in love   your private love
if the stars are fine
the floor remains in place

DALLY

the teeth of time   yes square   and grin
just emotion has them sharp   my soul
is haired   my skin has feelings   friends
surround me as a shroud   would body
break for me the sand   widening
pause and when I ask how long
it answers   oh not long   I had my phone
my cat   climbs up me when I was
reading   first pressure of the day is clawed
takes my lap up hisses the house then
hums   the windows let in news
if I feel it in a shift   my chair
annotates   and I am dumb
as candy in the fridge   a chill
not different from warmth
useless   when I pushed my empathy
into you   shared your sorrow
bared my guilt   the best self steps offstage
in clothes   not me   noisy loves you

weeps to it   can't overthrow me
rigid   the trace of temper in the juice
shellacks it into place

I'M WHAT NOW

I don't need to be healthy but I like
the smell of health, c'mere
I'll put my nose in your lily neck
now how lucky for how long
will I be in my dwelling
I feel the fugly luck of passing
by the right bridge in the rain
now when I lie on grass there's space
my body makes by grass's bending
if I lie here long I'll kill it all
and I'll be death's impressioner
now do I have to build a bench or learn
to sit more softly? Why
my body won't live long enough
in Spain or Philadelphia
Oakland or anywhere to feel I am
a native plant contributing
I don't like it but I feel alone
useless your parasite a parasite
of art and Philadelphia and earth

sometimes I don't brush my teeth
and I taste like dying and I die
or I feel like your imaginary friend
or I smell like you

FEARFUL EVEN

stamp the opposing evening
with two cat's eyes
a lapse in renewed position
not renewed
and the last task you meant to follow through
upon you didn't

one banner solid blue
and one unmarked by dye
set it to quake
to free my borrowed sky
when I'm another kind of animal
an under kind

so I unhand it
because I'm burrowing
leave my stump
sat upon by droopy sprouts
alone or dirt that's tired
that lacerates me but as a tattoo would

only parts made available
the heart's at school
always or drops out forever
see the issue with my messages
to land on a button
isn't a commitment

why's the arrow
anxious always
try in a thunderclap
alighting

FUCK YOU

silken clyster strike me clean
slip out sick milk and soak me blank
flatten my silver
pinken my blacken hole
for I've been awful
eaten & fucked
and sided with hypocrites and idled
nightly
skidded across tile
paid no mind to sidewalks
preened
stylishly for acres of velveteen
ever been born aloof
ever been siphoned in
lichen of dallied anywhere near liquid
fucked up
easily and snuck
my skinny lips in filth
and sucked

LOOKS TO AVOID

I think a rare
is a real
and I think you've got it
when it comes to you
bare the bird who flaps
bare the born human
padding with air and bare
the human neck unbreathing
the unventilated neck
bare the airy human being
and sacrifice
the unknit belly cords
a live known isn't
a mutant sex is separate
lack palms when holding
faceless when away

POEM ABOUT SEEDLESS TOMATOES AREN'T FRUIT

Let's beg a vegetable from the vendor,
a wet crabapple or a damp cucumber
and bring it home to murder with a cleaver.
You can't murder something dead
but you can't bring it home either.
Let's cut an apple on cut tree. Let's plate it.
Let's plate the statue in a limpid silver.
It represents the city's founding father.
He's a deity. Another deity becomes another.
I found my burgeoning on casual leverage,
seemingly casual springboarding of sprawling.
I land on someone sexy and I wet them.
I make them a damp catcher and I like it.
You should be grateful or be furious, depending.
Do you like it? My falling's calling to your catching.
Oh hear it with your arms out, likely listener.
batten up the clapboards and put snacks on,
plate windows with the steaming pies and sing it,
placate my skin with micturate and dust us clean
with powder, pee upon me friend

we'll dim our barricades, we're bargaining
to limit our toy weather. And we haven't yet
learned to not cook together. Let's eat our bubblewrap
with forks, how digestible, and when you want me
I'm at market, buying dairy, second ingredient
for a dish we get to suffer.

BROKE UP

I give up my lizard

yeah
go find heat buddy

I live in a *bank*
it's all like "water" I'm like "ca$h"
dammit $$$ so I don't sun
nor are there rocks to be upon

I have bosses
have bosses have

pulled through by noses

I'm a dry fish is how I met the lizard
yes lizard in the day's heat
pulsed and shone

and I was like "water"

"water" the bank said "*$$$$$*"
my nose was like "yes"
the liz was "what is it?"

I was alive to the emotion
I knew my breath was being held

liz goes
for me it has melted

all my lucre goes
teeter-totter on a scale

WAY UP LATE

but an eye swole
an eye to the uppermost

whole lip in a circle top
euet to the top part

what hoops to be a part o
sip what's about to

my bought honey my
purchases of luck

super elucidant emperor
lup

and I'm putted to a plastic
rest stop in the nice grass

my eye eye
look up

from little low lookit
whole body hovering

up above a bed
w/o me

one month of hover
to be up at night

very high up
not where the bed's

as the bed's not
where the love weighs

but she who lapse
lags lapse bereft
probably

who'd'll do to be
slotted in oily
alonety

one summer tightly
afloat like knots

help ropes bob
new lemon

one moan too
an eyewhite

WHEN RELINQUISH ON A STAR

of June singing, of Monday singing, of losing you by the wayside
    singing
I never noticed losing you Monday in June, tra la
of March singing, of relics singing
of bringing it home the first time singing
I invited you home to worry my mother, tra la

sweet treats in the crisper, lo mein on the counter for hours
biscuits I punched out of dough for the house to devour
of Rebecca singing, of the concert singing
of losing you at the concert singing
intermixing too rapidly for my sexual attention span tra la
of quickness singing, of sinning singing, of a longlost girl Friday I'm
    singing
my right hand disguising whatever my left hand was holding

I stay awake past the cusp of day, sing my not sleeping
you wore me out, leading me not quite from the crime
did I pee on the leafpile you leapt in
of sexual exhaustion singing, of the floor tiles, of June

did I get in the boat of your partner
of karaoke, I lobbed my wet eyes at your partner
I told you I meant all my mixing

of learning I'm toxic to you by your sudden reaction
burial of my flirt and the upturned earth of my bedsheets
burial of my wish the upturned earth of my bedsheets, of not
    sleeping
singing, of not ending to dream, waking up in June or October
escaping acquaintance by desperate means is a pleasure

but losing your day by the wayside can harm you at nightfall or
    dawn
snags your eyelids midcycle, I'm learning, singing
glittery boat drip, a thunderstorm rising past fenceposts I'm singing
of rising from roads into pitch sky and sticking, of packing
of August and skipping to demons sing lo
sorry 'bout the demons tra la

LOVELY HEART

I leave my wallet on the lawn
then my heart changes

blue wire in the grass
red wire yellow wire sic

my brother Sam
make sparkles

break
born clean

but got dirt on though
a money holds me

home and house together
else my home'd

fit in my mother
clipped grass does wet

tally on my bare leghairs
certainly green my wet

wallet
housed feels

skulled uh
opinions

I can buy carelessness

but I can't unimplicate that action

oh and I can't buy freedom
but I can denude my wishlist

and get just
very personal

with my favorites
I don't know

is polyamory anticapitalist

or is it she said greedy
I said sure

and generous
so generous

as to take the self apart

to lie under my lovers fucking
being like

it's what it's like
to be a back

WHAT NIGHT

this is the part after you find yourself
not the hero but the sacrifice
where you decide your people
deserve you and enter the room now
                    good move
where you tell your mother she
is more beautiful than traveling
your words are beautiful moreso than truth
it's not too hot in the Inland Empire
                    at night
                        blankets
use your hands to tell a long story
wherein not much happens but some jokes
find yourself become abrupt
like a freaky old professor
where in your career you've already
shrunk in place and drinking wine it stays
                    the flush
                    good story
wherein you get really knocked up

after a night imprinted badly
hide the child in wood
                    how free
about when you still bleed quarter time
when what happens at home necessarily
        stays between sheets
in the squat you wake with it caked in your skirt
go to meet a friend
                to find
you've become colleagues

STATUARY

severely darkened
rerouted motorbike to be a yard standard
the boyfriend who went out of round
if personhood is shaped by persons
we don't do a solid job of it
love's temporary like an infant
if shapes are meant by motion
the motorbike's a lawn gnome now
same class marker but not adorable
fairies steal babies and leave toddlers
the infant's brain knits a new person

oh a new person a new person
in the evening the lopsided curtain
proves the street lit
lights the one who got around to it
tucking dark in at the corners
sleep should be plentiful for anyone
canopied in metal
this planet's for the gang of us

luxe and yawning
refuge from unendurable talk
promises and gossip
revert to spooning

me as middle
a lover coils
of me in small hours
reckoning
time till I'm pliant
and unwield and make
sweet lover giving vocals

the wet lips
heated sweetheart
saying sweetheart as the curtain fails
and day menages in

FREE TIME

I am getting into the car that will take me
to Southern California where I have family
all my family holds it up in a hot slophouse
this beats going out of your mind
it beats paying attention too much to planning
is this entry of a car that swings forward
I like it to go toward my family but not yet
be with them
parked in front of the yard and my Pop exits
the house my Mom exits the house and my brother
inside is my sister too many pets I like that
but first I'll get in the car and be glided
yes I like the fields I have never touched them
dust flies to be near me
but it has never come up
at my touch or delineated
me in the knuckles

I take long vacations
for small cash

with my friends sing
along in the front seats
the fields are busy they do not come to meet us
they are not really for us to touch
my filth is most parts my own body surfacing
scales sift down
my friends drive I never learned to touch wheels
behind me my old frights ahead all my family
and my old frights above me
a lover whom I have not seen in a while and won't
words from them pour in my cup
I hear it

I love them this I have learned how to do
and sing with my driving friends

how could anybody be so lucky?
how could anybody never do a job that wasn't loving?
that didn't sound good? that wasn't clean?
how could anybody sit back and move forward?
there is no fairness obviously "brothers
I snooze while you sweat" Anaïs Nin made Henry Miller
erase from his manuscript

IN DEFENSE OF MUFFIN

I have lived at home and am ready
again to take up that
mantle of fantastic privilege
if all our differences are cliffs
it's better
to be brave than right   probably
over time
I learn to take up space with hair
share opinions and I'm told
I'm defensive then to defend
that   that what I said
wasn't a response it just
came second no one asked it
it arrived just as you arrived
but who is my opinion to complain?
I'm alive I have beautiful legs
and I've never worked at all
my thoughts
are free like ducks
in the park provided   I could die

anytime unsolicited it would be hard
to stop me   who are you and I
to leave a difference in one
another? It is just that we are free
so to know what to take down
from the day is a begot skill
we had to invent surfaces
to get busy I am so busy with you
so you draw me
up from where I sink
when I want
where the pond averages green
I have bobbed in it
and my brain's made more snaps
readier
for the prism happening in that
wow that water in the sky

OFFER HONOR

I try to order honor
I would ford a river

But as a drop I just succumb in water
In flight I bent my finger

My arms bear my conjecture
I rushed a minute earlier

Unduly rough when speaking to my daughter
She writes a mental letter

Asking me not to wait for dusk to lower
I say okay to her

But I don't like to hear the words together
People couple to suffer

Luck is what dents the record
and Love is no survivor

Families part but roofs withstand most weather
I make my home in architecture

ANDERERWAY

when it pushes shadow from the trees
and presses it from their needles outside the Dey House
and the bus is dark inside   when it picks apart the lawn
and you are here
will you soften me?   for the sun
will you deflect it?
I am blinking in the atrium   the library
I don't know if you have a room for me
or where on me you can lie down

but I want my anger easily exhausted
the way fact takes the rug from an argument
we both go on the floor
I do feel your shade
your wavy boughs   you dream
you are leaving me
I would become an ordinary person if you did
but you are awake   and I am ordinary anyway
and it pushes through me

DUMBSHOW

the mayor is a secret king
egg shines upon his pan
ever the good answer
in his hands he sweats it

pats it   loose fruit husk
my idiot's   my sex
my deity's   in touch with it
the area outside my box
is public information
because famous

root for the conductor
with his grin
fruit softens at the pit
the mayor unravels
himself   dimpling
yes his jacket's cusp
undoes

but no one else is fancy
no one knows   the mayor
is handsomest   unjacketed
and shirtless   undershirtless
jeweled crowned

SEEN THROUGH

window that tired old subject
just about as tired as mirror

as tired as sky I see that sky
I sort of know I see through

the sky blows out whitening

the idea of my mirror gnaws
the idea of Sophia in this glass

or glassy screen assembled
did I mean written never

written in light so not written
projected says the windowpane

now we live on the third floor
I am trying to get blank daily

perhaps just to see I can't
to see what sweeps across me

when I am at the store or home
I still speak as if cavernous

as if streams pertained to me
though now I'm eye to eye with air

I think the sky has what to do
inside the fan works its winding

wool compounds our bed's heat

I'm so hot I think I'm summer
or I think my mood is weather

the trees behind the houses bend
like too polite to disagree

you come home soon that
makes the door beat

FOCI FOCI

I don't even know what to do
when I'm not drawing your face

engines drop from cars
and cars roll

I can't begin to stand
without my feet mixing

it's that Saturday feeling
that ruffles my lungs

makes my hands static
dipping and gliding
the bluebirds

sucking and spitting
mouths of some creatures
like people

I go rooting up
softness from exes

then glimmery distrust

a white wave pokes
from a blue continuum

I go my sweetheart sleeping
on a becandled mattress

all his hopes
single out someone

blowy heater
locus of supplement

heal a split lip
the wind won't

and I backup when the wind steps
just in front of me

drowsy lips
and nasal barricade

with suffering
I can manage

putting down a pen
but I don't know what to do then

OH HEAR WET NOISE

gates break to let in
beauteous new air
the beds get antsy
crumby in the cover
curly in the corner
on the window smears
the person pawed
upon it not looking
or looking in

view boils away
to catch the smudge
boils back to hear
bright gate cracking
laminated midday
mood walking up it
blight and blonde path
buds up the weedy
watery noise is here
wetter noise nearby

OVERS

on my plate

again

tomato

over my big lip my thin lip
over which my philtrum's
learned to twitch of late

tell me about it
face

I've got no object way to quell
this nervousness
it gets me in my skin

when I have two things
food and a plate

I can take those things apart

but this

what's up I can't be certain
sure it's just as like
unpleasant as its symptoms

like to like of it
my shiver's roots

might be in my red heart

maybe or my yellow
gut or my backless gown

my yawn
a symptom of my night
my night a symptom

POEM A DAY

poem a darling
sweet dear
a blue
awhile now
lurk but jangling
whose argument
shook the bushes
ours
but the reality
may be
as it drops to a floss
below us
at least below our choices

plead a took word
to return a promise
with a compliment
shakes the plane to sloping

a sleek watered limb
allows us forward
swap a nice moment
for clarity
brute sweetheart

bright brute heart
wet
and what lopes between
pulled taut but dropped
then to lure
one a dear
who in a rush
is darling

MY HEART BUOYS WHEN I BUHOLD

own heart
to release backstroke
pawprints up a
tongue a gut
leaps to solitude

oh once the ocean
twice my love the sea
and dissolves
pants laundered
tidily to the body
dissipates
blood to the corners
soften the want
is not neat
rafted wander
there's no way

oh but the bent
love at the

back the mobile
spots on
him the heart's
own boy

JUST YOU & ME & OUR THIRD EYE

blanching in daylight
and it swarms together
pulls apart
in buds
twitch in the overlap
where you color
and I do
so the flower shifts in place
I'd like to stream
the eye
I see
your little palm fits in me
deep
and pulls a river down

OH H

FOR BROOKE CENA

like a carousel of pegasi
mortared in honey
does my baby turn

like a chandelier flexing
light through chimes
and baubles does my baby shake
toting
attention upwards like a god
or some god's carrier does my boo
rotate upon my palm

like a carousel
of pegasi mortared
in honey

DID IT HURT THO

the sun is out for good
the snow is halving

half of my heart is homeland

half is mustard
I make the most of it

normal and blooming
all yellow's best
you say

I knew for once
things that my heart could do

not follow a bus
or turn over in hand
my heart

waits until floating
that's the manna of it

manna's out in the sun
falls from the sky

like you did

like you did
before you were mine

SHELL OUT

due to a white beach you find
me here home
dug up all stark
my armpits
cling sand
sun speaks
rude remembrance out my forehead

sun fucked sun
sky fucked sky
earth all earthfucked and the sea
too skins the shore
my personable each to each
never did suffice to make it
only a fine day

a damp dying
crust
salt and pepper in the wild meal
out of a mind
a mixture

I would like one true
oil one true
lemon or vinegar
some fingering thing
to pick the summer out the vegetable

chase the taste across the table
limp against
the uncouth radish
too radiant

colors to meet a white bed
white ceiling
red ass me between
at the sand and sea
and sun in a wet-dry
variant

heat and my home
faltered and fell inside me
when two fins slipped out

INCY

and I have been dented by it

I have lain and looked into the ceiling
and the tiles have stirred

while the trees bent
the wind in
I have swum in my clothes

gripping counters have leaned
and my neck has rolled
I have loaned

attention as my scalp
sweated the very tip of me
I was and the din

ate the gasp I lost
standing

and I have bitten the arm of the couch

and left holes
I have lain on my own back and this
it has sat on me

(TRUE)

eclipse to be
new weather

what snaps in the holding
of together
undergrows
the lived with obvious
&the forgotten dream

who would not say
holding is worthy
is an adherent
nonetheless
gravity
even as it compounds us
gives us toys

rest & sincerity
or their possibility

(((((((((((((()))))))))))))))

in winter   pancakes
in the summer's butter
spring in witches better
autumn's what the summer must
I take it up with time
and season wheats me

homey weather sacks the soup
the bucks are anywhere
but anyone who lived for art
died poor or married rich
which would be the death of me
I fold in the library
my patent shoes scallop to heel
to toe the dance they choose
the beverage was clearly there
not a drink if standing

in document   reverb
in the West   a goose

the bad tree that fell toward me
followed me into me
we made reverse dryad
and they teased it out of my skin

in heartthrob   bebop
in leggings   lakes
in me the dual runnings of a one
a two who wants to be
more freely yours the magma
hops the new year
earneth over

ACKNOWLEDGMENTS

"Tandem," "All Out of Doors," and "Legroom" appeared in *BOMB*. "When Relinquish on a Star" appeared in *The Awl*. "Prismr of Love," "I'm a Ninny," "Let Go Swimming," and "Lovely Heart" appeared in *The Recluse*. "Time Check," "What Night," and "Dally" appeared in *Poor Claudia*. "In Defense of Muffin" appeared in *Lambda Literary*. "Anyone Must Sand Gingers" appeared in *LVNG*. "Offer Honor" appeared in *Dusie*. "Oh H" appeared in *Textsound*. "Foci Foci" appeared in *The Volta*. "Way Up Late" and "Blur Anise" appeared in *Denver Quarterly*. "I'm a Natural," "Shell Out," and "Just You & Me & Our Third Eye" appeared in *Tupelo Quarterly*. "Oh Hear Wet Noise," "Overs," and "Incy" appeared in *STILL*. "When I'm Reeking It Could Break or It Could Be Unseemly or Egregious or a Bunny" appeared in *Fence*. "(True)," "Ponder the Lily How Does it Go," "I'm What Now," and "(((((((((((((((())))))))))))))))" appeared in *Supplement*. "Poem a Day" and "Poem About Seedless Tomatoes Aren't Fruit" appeared in *Berkeley Poetry Review*. "Andererway" was featured on the Poetry Foundation's *PoetryNow* and *Poem a Day* podcasts.

Thank you to my parents, Per and Don. I love you. So too do I love and thank my sister Rose and brother Sam and our very large family.

Thank you poets of the Bay Area for teaching me to be a writer in the world. Thanks especially to Brandon Brown for helping me shape the final draft of this book.

Thank you to my grad & undergrad professors, Joan Retallack in particular, and my fellow students and your inspiring criticisms.

Thank you, Garrett Caples and the City Lights team.

The state of the world calls out for poetry
to save it. LAWRENCE FERLINGHETTI

CITY LIGHTS SPOTLIGHT SHINES A LIGHT ON THE WEALTH
OF INNOVATIVE AMERICAN POETRY BEING WRITTEN TODAY.
WE PUBLISH ACCOMPLISHED FIGURES KNOWN IN THE
POETRY COMMUNITY AS WELL AS YOUNG EMERGING POETS,
USING THE CULTURAL VISIBILITY OF CITY LIGHTS TO BRING
THEIR WORK TO A WIDER AUDIENCE. IN DOING SO, WE ALSO
HOPE TO DRAW ATTENTION TO THOSE SMALL PRESSES
PUBLISHING SUCH AUTHORS. WITH CITY LIGHTS SPOTLIGHT,
WE WILL MAINTAIN OUR STANDARD OF INNOVATION AND
INCLUSIVENESS BY PUBLISHING HIGHLY ORIGINAL POETRY
FROM ACROSS THE CULTURAL SPECTRUM, REFLECTING
OUR LONGSTANDING COMMITMENT TO THIS MOST
ANCIENT AND STUBBORNLY ENDURING FORM OF ART.

CITY LIGHTS SPOTLIGHT

Printed in the USA
CPSIA information can be obtained
at www.ICGtesting.com
JSHW082222140824
68134JS00015B/689